C000110053

Other titles in this series
(all by Susan Quilliam):

# Body Language Secrets: Success at Work

*Susan Quilliam*

Thorsons
*An Imprint of* HarperCollins*Publishers*

Thorsons
An Imprint of HarperCollins*Publishers*
77–85 Fulham Palace Road,
Hammersmith, London W6 8JB
1160 Battery Street,
San Francisco, California 94111-1213

Published by Thorsons 1996
10 9 8 7 6 5 4 3 2 1

A catalogue record for this book
is available from the British Library

ISBN 0 7225 3125 7

Printed in Great Britain by
Woolnough Bookbinding Limited, Irthlingborough

*To Desmond Morris – who else?*

# Contents

# Acknowledgements

I would first like to acknowledge the many sources and individuals who helped me gain my research material, particularly the staff of the Open University Library, the staff of the University of London Library, and Felicity Sinclair. A special acknowledgement to Samantha Smeraglia for her ability to collate my research so wonderfully!

My thanks also to: Barbara Levy, my agent, for her continued support; Sharon Scotland, the illustrator; to Jane Graham-Maw, Michele Turney, Jenni Maas and Barbara Vesey from

Thorsons for making the writing and
production of this book such an enjoyable
experience; to my personal assistant June
Bulley for her constant administrative
excellence.

A final thank you to my husband Ian who, as
always, makes all things possible.

Throughout this book, the people referred to
could be either 'he' or 'she'. Consistently
referring to one gender would not only raise
political issues, but would be unfair to the
'other kind'! In general, therefore, unless to do
otherwise would make the text inaccurate,
I have alternated pronouns in successive
questions in this book, to give a balanced feel.

# Preface

Before you read this book, remember that body language:

- is every kind of human behaviour *except* the words spoken – from gestures to breathing, from the way muscles move to a person's use of time
- is not able to tell you everything – you may need the words too
- does not let you read everyone like a book – because everyone has his or her own personalized body language
- will not give you power over people – they will not respond unless they want to

- will not work if you try to change others
  – you can only ever shift what *you* do and
  alter the situation that way
- is about gathering information – you will
  be more successful if you do
- is something you already know – your
  natural body language works best
- is best tried out slowly and carefully – new
  body language patterns can look false
- works by trial and error: do more of what
  succeeds, and stop doing anything that
  doesn't!

## How Can Body Language
## Help Me Succeed at Work?

A lot of research into body language has been funded by – and so focused on – the business world. Therefore there is already a huge body of knowledge within the field of nonverbal communication about the strategies for career success.

Whatever your field – whether you are a skilled worker, an office worker, a manager or a creative wizard – body language can help. First, it shows you what to look for in order to understand your own workplace and your own particular work situation. It helps you analyse what is really going on under the surface, the hidden rules that you need to follow in order to succeed with your colleagues, your employees, your managers, your boss.

Based on these rules, body language then gives you the strategies you need to be able to play the system. It helps you present yourself in a way that will impress – in what you do, what you say, how you act, how you interact. And, as it is sometimes difficult to tell when you are impressing and when not, body language helps further by helping you to read the nonverbal judgements on your performance given by colleagues, customers and clients.

Finally, you will recognize that in business, whether deliberately or through oversight, honesty is not always the only policy. Clients can be unaware of what you need to know; opponents can bend the truth. Body language can help by allowing you to spot what they will not tell you.

In short, body language can allow you to read the secret code behind the words. And that will always give you the edge in your career.

## What Does My Workplace Say About the Company I Work for?

Like it or not, your workplace reflects your employers. They will choose the building itself, organize the layout of the workspace, order the furniture and fittings – all to indicate what is important to them and what they want to be important to you.

Is wealth the main aim? There is an accountancy firm in the City of London where the custom-built building is like a fortress. It even has a mock-portcullis and a little gatehouse where you need to check in before visiting. The foyer is huge, lined with marble, and has a picture on the wall that obviously cost more than the average mortgage. This is a firm where money matters, where customers want to be shown that there is real wealth and where the nonverbal signals the firm gives are aimed to reassure and to inspire confidence.

If it is hierarchy that is most vital in your company, watch for the status icons. Directors will have desirable office locations on higher floors, with more windows, more space and more secretaries. They have all the trappings of kingship, such as throne-like swivel chairs with high backs, or a huge, altar-like desk with a reflective surface that will seem to increase the size of the owner's presence. And of course, any company where the managers back-bite about which level of car they are allowed to have is making a nonverbal statement that it is a hierarchical organization.

What if group co-operation is the most important aim? A people business, such as advertising or the media, may use open-plan offices to reinforce co-operative working. There will be perhaps a hundred same-size desks per office, designed to reinforce the view that everyone is equal and can both see and hear each other equally. At the side of this arena there will be lots of dedicated meeting spaces with round tables so that everyone can see each other. There will be a telephone on every desk, and even if the bosses have their own offices they will be glass-walled and will have doors that are jammed permanently open.

Which are more important, the 'customers' or the staff? Compare a supermarket or shop, where the majority of the work area is devoted to the 'punters' and the brightly lit shelves, wide aisles and sparkling customer toilets contrast with the glimpse of tatty shelving or torn-down posters you may get when a 'staff only' door swings open. On the other hand, is yours the kind of company which rarely sees the client, where there actually is not a seat to sit on at reception, and an outsider has to shift uneasily from one foot to another until the employee he has come to see wedges another chair beside the desk so that the visitor can sit down?

Whichever general style your workplace follows, you probably cannot change it. But what you can do, not only out of interest but also with the aim of getting ahead, is to use your analysis of that general style to understand more about the company that employs you – and about the values it stands for.

## How Can I Customize My Workspace to Meet My Needs?

Does your workspace actually help you work? Is the space the right size? Too little can feel cramped and constricting and can make you feel uncomfortable and distracted. Too much space to work in, as when you are in an open-plan office, may make you feel insecure. If you cannot erect screens, then perhaps you can build your own 'sanity protectors' with stacked files, books or equipment.

Is the furniture right? Whatever kind of work surface you have, you should be able to reach things easily and without strain. Adjust your chair height and buy a footrest if necessary, so that your back is supported and you can move freely. But do not have too comfy a chair, otherwise your body will unwind too much and you will never feel alert at work. And use your workspace to assist what you do: perhaps angling the chairs towards each other if meetings are a large part of your work, turning your desk firmly towards a blank wall if your job demands mostly head-down concentration.

Is yours a noisy environment? Complete silence can be unnerving, but too much noise affects performance because, in a very real sense, you cannot hear yourself think. So unless you are in a job that uses only your physical and not your mental talents (in which case turn up the canned music or take a Walkman to work), reduce the volume – using earplugs if necessary.

Work lighting needs to be bright enough to keep you awake. Slightly dimmed lighting makes you more likely to talk, but less inclined to do physical work or to concentrate. Very dim lighting with a single bright spot shining directly on your desk will conversely make you less likely to talk but better able to concentrate on the job in hand – a system used in one London translation bureau which presumably wants to encourage its staff to focus on the work they are doing, but not to talk among themselves!

Think about warmth. Most companies nowadays know the health and safety regulation that, once the temperature drops below 16°C (61°F), workers cannot be expected to work productively and must be sent home. Fewer firms know that if the temperature goes too high this creates irritation in a workforce, and that a regular temperature dampens spirits. So open the window (if there is one!) if the room gets too hot, and try to take regular breaks in the open air.

Finally, you may want to meet other, less purely professional needs. You may want to keep plants in the office, install a coffee machine on the desk, have your six-year old's latest drawing pinned up on the wall. It is motivating to imprint your personality on your work environment – though, before you do, check that it does not clash with the company culture. One British advertising agency actually instructs its cleaners to bin any personal belongings found on employees' desks at night! So observe your office culture carefully and personalize just the amount that is likely to help you make the right impression.

## Are There Any Hard-and-fast Guidelines About How I Should Look at Work?

Here is a sobering thought: A survey of 300 top personnel directors said that they judged a potential employee, or someone they were thinking of promoting, mainly on the basis of her (or his) appearance. Performance counted, but the bottom line was that if a person did not look right, then she did not get ahead.

So how should you look? The rulebooks and style guides make it all seem very simple: you need to dress to look attractive and well groomed, you need to dress formally and smartly.

But however many style guides you read, you can still go wrong. For 'looking right' varies from company to company, even from department to department. And this is true whether or not a 'uniform' is part of your job – as it is if you are in the armed forces or medicine. It is true whether or not there are formal dress codes laid down – as there are on the shop floor. Above and beyond these formal codes, every group of people will have developed its own informal style rules. You may not be aware of it, particularly if you are new, but this secret dress code will be there.

This code will partly depend on the nature of your business. Media jobs often encourage you to dress fashionably and brightly, while money jobs prefer conservative dress in dark colours. The code will also depend on your status within a business: the office junior can

often wear jeans, the directors cannot. The code will shift with your gender: women are usually allowed to wear more fashionable and colourful clothes than are men. It may even vary according to your department: perhaps the sales force wears suits while the computer team wears chinos.

In fact, this code may actually totally contradict the style guide rules. Wear safe business garb in a creative environment and you may seem boring and without potential. Get your hair coloured, however subtly, for your job in a traditional provincial solicitors' firm and you may be labelled a bimbo (male or female).

The fact is that you have to make any dress decision according to what you personally see around you in the work situation you are in.

So check out not what you *think* should happen, but what *actually* happens, in regard to: suit or not; skirt or trousers; dark colours, primaries or pastels; formal or casual; tie pattern, shape and colour; fashion style; jewellery; hair cut; makeup.

Check out too how the rules change in different situations – if you are working out of the office; if you are seeing a client; if you are on site. Check out how the style subtly shifts as one head of department succeeds another who has a totally different style approach. And keep checking. The long painted nails that were acceptable last year may well be seen as tacky this year. The button-down shirt that was the height of fashion when you started in the job may be a black mark on your appraisal by the time you are through your probationary period.

## How Can My Body Language Help Me Fit in at Work?

If you are working with other people, then of course you have to be friendly to them. And so you will probably want to use the kind of body language that will make them feel good about you and vice versa.

Psychologists have identified patterns of body language that achieve this, called 'immediacy' patterns. Immediacy body language includes facing people directly, looking at them, leaning towards them as they speak, having a friendly expression, smiling. You probably know and use all these signals regularly in your social life.

But beware using them inappropriately at work. At work, you need to get the job done and not confuse the issue with too much friendly feeling. So tone down your immediacy with more formal body language. Do not approach too close. Do not smile, giggle or laugh overmuch. And tone down any expression of negative emotion, such as tears or tantrums, that might draw any of your colleagues into a more personal relationship with you.

That said, of course the rules do vary. Some companies are comfortable with very immediate body language, others prefer a very formal style. Some departments, such as creative ones, tend to be more immediate in their nonverbal approach than others. Some people – such as clients and managers – will by their presence shift the body language temporarily; the noise level will spontaneously go down and employees will be less likely to visit each other's desks, drop things or lean back in their chairs.

And some specific situations call for different body language approaches. After a company catastrophe, such as redundancies or a big drop in sales, then immediacy will rise – you may well move close to each other, touch to comfort or show strong emotion, at least until the crisis is over. At the other end of the scale, in a promotion interview you will almost certainly be more formal than you otherwise would be, even towards colleagues with whom you are normally quite friendly. Once the interview is over and your promotion has been announced, on the other hand, you may celebrate by hugging and kissing!

## What Is the Pecking Order at Work, and Why Should I Worry About It?

In any group of birds, some get to peck the corn first, others later. A group of birds will arrange themselves in an informal but strict status hierarchy – the 'pecking order'. And so will any group of humans.

If the group is a work team or department, then very often the formal boss or manager is at the top of the pecking order – if not, then he (or she) will find it hard to keep control and command. But even if everyone in a group is equal in terms of salary and status, its members will take up a personal pecking

order – which may have nothing to do with
work values. Being top may be about being
married, being fashionable, having children or
being the one who throws parties, just as
much as about being good at the job, working
hard or being next in line for promotion.

Pecking order is not something you talk
about. It may not even be something most
people are conscious of. But everyone in a
particular group will unconsciously reflect the
pecking order by his or her body language. So,
for example, there will be a totally unspoken
order of who gets precedence in conversation.
Who speaks first? Who can speak for longest
without interruption? Who is allowed to
interrupt whom, and who has to shut up if
interrupted? Who can change the subject, who
can close the conversation?

Another pecking order clue is who has control over space. So who pops into whose office without knocking, leans over another person's desk, shifts other people's belongings without permission? Who can take over filing cabinets without permission? Who can take over the corner of the car park with his camper van without anyone else complaining?

Often, pecking order is about who does things and who has things done for him. And this is one reason why, in order to make managers seem higher in the pecking order, they often have assistants to help them. The lower in the pecking order you are, the more you will be expected to make the tea, go out for sandwiches, fetch and carry. But it does work both ways – if you are high in the pecking order, you may be expected to play 'lord (or lady) bountiful' – lending your possessions or inviting others to dinner. It is expected, for example, for a boss to buy a 'round' in a situation where the office junior just would not – unless it were your birthday, an occasion which immediately raises you in the pecking order, just for the day!

What if someone steps outside his pecking order? Then, as if by magic the whole group will unconsciously close ranks against the upstart. If you interrupt someone above you in the pecking order, then he will just talk over you and the group will stare you down. If you walk without knocking into the office of someone above you in the pecking order, you will receive a frosty stare, if not an actual reprimand. So be aware of what the pecking order is in your company – and tread carefully. It could make the difference between being accepted and being ostracized!

## How Can Body Language Help Me Steer Clear of 'Office Politics'?

Most office politics boils down to 'who sides with whom?' To avoid getting caught up in the conflict, first spot the groups that are siding with each other.

Every group will nonverbally signal its identity. Members of one group may display what are called 'tie' signs, signals that they identify with each other. They may wear the same kind of suit. They may encourage each other to have their hair styled the same way. They will all go off for a smoke together. They will mark out little areas as their 'territory', pushing desks together, gathering at the same table in the canteen, perhaps even placing actual barriers, such as a filing cabinet or a plant, at the entrance to their area of the workspace.

This group identity may differ from that of another group in the same office. Look for slightly different styles of dress, one group wearing jeans while the other wears leggings. Look for different activities, one group going down to the pub while the other brings in sandwiches. Already, you have the foundations of opposition.

But do you have hostility? In work situations, people often try to hide what they really feel, so the signals may be subtle. Look for an absence of normal social contact: do the members of one group hang back from

visiting the desks of the other? When they do,
do they scarcely smile, rarely stop and chat,
keep their remarks short and brusque? Do
they lean backwards, keep a blank expression,
shake their heads fractionally when listening
to the others talk? You may notice 'leakages'
of hostility – unconscious, fleeting facial
expressions of anger or frustration coming
through the normally bland and friendly
working mask.

Can you steer clear of all that? It can be
difficult, because you may well naturally side
with one group rather than the others – and
your body language may reveal this whether
you want it to or not. But if tension in your
work situation is such that you need to tread a
determinedly neutral path, then you have to
behave towards all sides in a way that shows
equal nonverbal approval. So balance out any

'tie' signs that bind you with any particular side; wear jeans one day and leggings the next. Avoid any activities that seem to demonstrate loyalty; if one group invites you to the wine bar, then be sure to go to the gym next day with another. Chat with members of all groups. When you pass on the corridor, give everyone the same friendly smile.

You could almost do a mental check at the end of each day: Have you spent as much time, with as many members, of each of the opposing groups? If not, then tomorrow redress the balance.

## How Can I Stand Up to the Office Bully?

Every company has an office bully, even if the other members of staff keep her (or him) under control. The bully is not likely to be a high-status person; more likely she (or he) is someone who is unsure of herself, but hides that with bluster. Look perhaps for a person whose slumped shoulders and downturned mouth tell you that she feels negative about life and will let that frustration out on others. Or look for someone whose slight swagger and sharp, aggressive tone of voice tell you that she would like to be leader of the pack – but not having the charisma of a natural leader, has settled instead for trying to dominate anyone who will let her do so.

For a bully is always someone who actually lacks self-esteem. Bullying boosts the bully's confidence by destroying someone else's. So whereas in a normal conflict at work you can usually resolve things by talking them through, with a bully this is not possible. Her only aim is simply to hurt – by calling names, by spoiling your work, sometimes by actual violence. And because of this, a bully will always choose to pick on people who look as if they will allow themselves to be hurt, will give up easily, will not fight back. The bottom line is that if your body language signals all these things, then you stand more of a chance of being bullied. If your body language instead signals self-confidence, then the bully may well leave you alone.

Begin by being aware of the particular set of body language signs that, in apes as well as humans, indicates 'loser'. Then make sure you are not showing any of these signs. Straighten your shoulders rather than hunching them. Look directly forward rather than away. Put aside nervous mannerisms, like chewing your hair, playing with your tie, scratching your head, smiling apologetically. Start mixing with colleagues who are also confident; a bully goes for loners, and will rarely tackle someone if he or she is surrounded by friends.

If the bully does approach you, stay calm. Do your best to ignore what is happening, taking a deep breath to remove tension, looking directly at the bully and, if you possibly can, simply acting as if she is a fool. The alternative is to go onto the attack: pull yourself up to full height, head up, look at the bully almost down your nose and keep your face serious – a smile can be a sign of appeasement as well as of amusement. In a loud, clear, angry voice tell her to go away. Then walk off.

If you are genuine and can really act as if the whole thing does not threaten you, then the bully will start to believe that you are not an easy victim. In the end she will look elsewhere, lose interest and forget you even exist.

## What Is the Secret Body Language of Sex at Work?

Lots of people fall in love at work. But because work is supposed to be about business rather than intimacy, often lovers have to hide their relationship – particularly if, as sometimes happens, one partner or both are already committed elsewhere! So sex at work is often secret. How can you spot it?

If you are with someone you suspect of being lovesick, watch him (or her) as the possible object of affection appears. Unconsciously, he will actually look spontaneously more

attractive; his muscle tone will increase, his lips will become slightly fuller – even the bags under his eyes may go down! He will automatically begin to show off his best points – turn his head to show a 'best side', pull in his stomach, sit up straight to show off broad shoulders (or full female breasts if the unrequited lover is female). He may start 'preening', improving his appearance by adjusting his collar, smoothing back his hair, licking his lips – (or as one group of young men were seen to do when a certain female manager entered the room, all straightening their ties in unison!).

As time goes by, you may then watch fascinated as both parties in the potential love relationship start to recognize their mutual attraction and to signal it to each other. Even if they think they are hiding what is happening, there will be subtle signs typical of people in love (or in lust). They will hold eye contact, looking more than usual and with less blinking than normal. They will use a slightly different tone of voice (low and husky) with each other than with any other colleagues. They may reveal a tendency to block off other people from intruding on their developing relationship by turning their backs to the room when they are together, or failing to see or hear attempts to interrupt their conversation.

Suddenly, a few days later, all these signals seem to stop. The lovers ignore each other on the corridor, exchange only polite greetings in the lift. Their expressions are completely blank, or even slightly hostile. They may begin to disagree with each other in a way they never did before. What is happening?

Possibly they have tried to create a relationship and it has failed. Their body language reflects the fact that they feel angry with each other and are trying to erase the memory. But it could be the total opposite: their relationship may have gone beyond flirting and they do not want anyone else to spot just how far it has gone.

So check the couple's unconscious body language signals. Are they still 'pointing' to each other with their bodies – elbows, feet, hand gestures all indicating the other person? Have they begun to 'match' each other, taking up the same body positions, using the same gestures at the same time, picking up the same turns of phrase?

If they are displaying these real signs of intimacy, then ignore the seeming hostility. It is a smoke screen to put observant people like you off the scent!

## How Does the Way I Use My Time Affect How My Colleagues See Me?

Your use of time makes a powerful nonverbal statement in your work situation every day about how efficient you are, how committed you are and how important you think you are.

The most basic statement you make is whether you are on time or not. Most companies see latecomers as also being inefficient and bad at their job, whether or not they are – and even if you are operating a flexitime system, there will be a cut-off time such as eleven o'clock, after which you will be judged as late even if you worked until midnight the day before.

But strangely, being early at work can also make a negative statement. Coming in to work early may indicate that you cannot handle your responsibilities within the normal 9-to-5 day. Arriving more than a quarter of an hour early for a meeting can indicate that you haven't got anything else important to do – and therefore that you are not doing an important job. And getting through a job too quickly and handing it in ahead of schedule can make people feel you have not done it well enough.

If you are paid by the hour and do overtime, the main statement this makes is that you need the money. If you are on salary, however, working after hours gets you noticed. Studies have shown that those who stay late in the evening tend to be seen as more central to the company, get consulted more about decisions, and are more likely to get promotion. On the other hand, in some companies working late is the norm, not the exception. Then if you do *not* stay late you are seen as slacking, and will get passed over for promotion even if, on paper, you are doing your statutory 40 hours and getting all the required work done on time.

The higher up you are in a company, the more you can misuse the time of others. At the bottom of the ladder your time is not your own, but your boss'. At the very top other people's time is at your disposal. You can extend meetings to suit you, change the timing of events, ask others to work late, tell them to come in early. You can keep them waiting in an outer office for hours – or days. You can be unavailable. The nonverbal message in the work situation is that the more important you are, the more valuable is your time compared to that of others.

## How Can I Be More Effective on the Telephone?

Body language is not just about what you see, but also about what you hear. The volume of a voice, its speed, tone, rhythm, pitch, accent and stress will all give you information about the person on the other end of the line. And your voice will affect your caller, making her (or him) more likely to co-operate with you – or not.

Use body language initially to make sure that you sound positive on the phone. If you are slumped in a chair with your head down, or if you are tense while phoning, you will sound tired; if your throat is restricted, research has shown that you may also sound insincere. On the other hand, a trick used by telesales people is to sit up and smile; your more cheerful physical state will transmit itself through your voice. Of course you may not be able to stand up during every phone call, but you can always sit up straight, and yawn beforehand to relax your jaw muscles.

Next, as you start the call and exchange greetings, listen carefully to the voice of the person on the other end of the phone. This allows you to pick up, from her tone of voice, just what sort of person she is and what kind of mood she is in. Is this an impatient customer, with a rushed, high tone of voice; a calm client with a slow, even speed? What does the stress she puts on different words tell you about what is important to her in what you are discussing?

Notice particularly if the caller's voice changes. For often, way before someone's words reveal that her mood or attitude has altered her voice will reveal this. A caller whose voice suddenly rises may be starting to get irritated. A caller whose voice suddenly drops, or who starts to hesitate between words, is perhaps becoming unsure. If you spot this, you can alter your approach to suit.

Really successful telephone talkers go one step further: They not only analyse the person they are talking to from her voice cues, they also spontaneously 'match' the other person's voice. You may have found yourself doing this with someone who has a strong regional accent – and then felt embarrassed at appearing to be mimicking her. In fact, this kind of spontaneous copying is barely noticeable to the listener and, as imitation is the sincerest form of flattery, can

58

actually be quite reassuring. So although it is unwise to do so deliberately, if you find yourself picking up on your caller's voice patterns, then you may well find that things go better.

Be aware of when the other person wants to end the call. Her speed may increase as if to hurry things up – or alternatively you may notice longer and longer silences between words. On the other hand, you may sense from the caller's tone of voice and a slight intake of breath down the line, that she has something more to say; stay on the line and give her the chance to do that.

Finally, make sure that the last words you speak sound cheerful, leaving the caller with a clearly positive impression of you.

## How Can I Best Meet My Clients' Needs?

Different clients want different things, above and beyond a good business deal. And if you do not meet their needs nonverbally, you may find yourself failing to satisfy without really knowing why.

Some clients like to be in charge. If you work in a service industry; your client may be used to having his demands met. He is the kind of person who has developed his own, controlling body language style to achieve this, looking serious and dominant, making leadership gestures that direct you round your own workspace, and using a clear voice that is completely at home with giving orders.

If what is important is keeping this client happy, then place him at the head of the table, in a high-backed chair; position yourself to one side. Keep standing until he sits, nod a good deal when he is speaking, let him feel in control because of your deferential body language.

But if what is important is to meet this client on equal terms – whether or not this destroys the deal – then shift the balance to a more equal one by sitting adjacent at a square meeting table; using chairs of equal-backed height; standing just as tall as he does; taking on a 'plus' expression (head erect, direct gaze and a neutral rather than placatory look on your face); and matching his dominant tone of voice with a firm, clear one of your own.

A second kind of client is one who needs to know that you are the expert. You are likely to be in a specialist industry, or selling a specialist product, and the client needs to rely on your knowledge. He may show his lack of certainty by a slightly nervous manner – or by a belligerence that is underpinned by nervousness. Underneath, he simply wants to be given the answers.

If you do have the knowledge and can provide a good service, then make sure that your body language reassures. Sit at the head of the table as if in charge, placing the client to one side. Stand to make your presentation, and use confident body language, your gaze direct, your gestures assured, your tone of voice firm and steady in a way that stresses your knowledge and capability. Use diagrams and charts to emphasizes that you know what you are doing well enough that you can put it down in black and white.

What about the client to whom personal contact is vital? If you are both in the people business, or in a co-operative profession rather than a competitive one, your client needs to feel good about you in order to do business with you. He will tend to call you by your first name, to ask about your personal life. He will use friendly body language, with smiles, easy gestures, meeting and parting hugs.

If you return your client's feeling for personal contact as the basis for professional dealings, then show this in your body language. Come down to the foyer to meet him and escort him personally to your office. Seat yourselves side by side or angled across a 'meeting sofa', then serve coffee, as you would to a friend. Notice yourself 'matching' or paralleling the way the client sits or moves – a sign that the two of you understand each other enough to copy one another spontaneously.

In short, however good the service you are offering, you also need to convince nonverbally. If you do, the client will be satisfied – and you will get repeat business.

## Can I Use Body Language Techniques to Achieve a Good Relationship with a Retail Customer?

Yes, you can. Use these techniques first to spot just the right moment to approach. Do not rush up to store customers who are 'just looking', as this can make them feel pressured. Instead, keep an eye on the customer who pauses at a particular item, reaches out and touches it, then perhaps picks it up so as to see it better. Just after this, there will be a precise moment when she (or he) looks around, eyebrows raised in an 'appeal look'. That is when she will welcome help, and that is when you can best start selling.

Begin by making contact. Look at the customer as you approach. Smile as you greet her – a universal signal of friendliness and reassurance. Then take up a position at an angle from her – directly opposite can seem too confrontational and creates a situation where you are seen as challenging the customer to buy.

Once having made contact, the tradition is to offer sales 'talk' – but it actually works better to use sales 'show', presenting your range to a customer and then reading her body language to judge what suits. As you do, develop the good relationship by making the customer the centre of your attention. Keep your focus on her, body, head and eyes all angled in her direction; turning away, looking away, speaking to someone else or fidgeting all give the nonverbal message that the customer and her purchase do not matter. Make your tone of voice warm, with interest and encouragement showing through. Do not smile too much once the first contact is made, as this can seem over-familiar, but keep a friendly expression – and an interested tilt of the head if that comes naturally to you.

If you can, give a brief touch. Place a hand on her arm while the customer is trying on a watch, a guiding hand to usher her into a changing room. Touching is one way to build good feeling, and studies have shown that sales assistants who touch a customer are three times more likely to achieve a sale. Timing is crucial, though; touch a person too soon and she will feel threatened, leave it too late and you will lose the effect.

Also be aware of the point where a customer starts to retreat. She may back off from the purchase and from her 'relationship' with you, perhaps because she is starting to get embarrassed for taking so long. She may start using 'blocking' body language, turning to one side, losing eye contact, placing her arms across her body, hugging a briefcase or bag for comfort. It can be tempting at this point to 'up the ante', but this will only make the customer feel pressured. Instead, wait with your attention still firmly on the customer, which may provide the nonverbal 'space' for her to get involved once again.

What if she doesn't? If she gives 'ready to go' signals, such as stepping back from the counter or looking towards the exit, then help her to leave – she will be far more likely to come back. Apologize for not

having what she needs, and say goodbye
with a smile that promises a welcome when
she returns.

## How Can I Really Tell When I Have Closed a Sale?

Whether your 'sale' is on the retail floor or in the boardroom, then it is useful to be able to tell whether you have closed it or not.

A customer or client thinking things through will probably fall silent for a few moments. If his (or her) eyes engage yours for a few seconds with a slight encouraging smile, then he is probably looking for input from you; if you tilt your head in enquiry, he may ask you the question he wants answered. If he turns and looks away from you, however, then he wants to consider the options alone.

A person still making his mind up also displays a number of 'indecision' signals. These usually involve some kind of imbalance, almost as if the person's body is 'weighing the options'. So you may notice a shake of the head from one side to the other, a wiggle of the shoulders, or a shift of weight from one foot to the other. One explanation of this is that the spinal cord, running down the centre of the body, carries signals to all parts – and if the signals are contradictory or uncertain, then this results in movement on first one side of the body, then the other. If you notice such imbalanced signals while a client is thinking, then do not interrupt.

When the thinking is done, and the client gives his answer, keep checking his body language – whether what he says is a 'yes' or a 'no'. For

sometimes what the client says may not be
what he means.

A client who says and means 'no' will usually
shake his head firmly as he utters the refusal.
Then he will be less likely to look you in the
eye, almost as if afraid of seeing any bad
reaction you may have. He will often try to
pull away and leave quite quickly, as if wary
that you will now pressure him. He will move
to the edge of his chair immediately and start
making gestures towards the exit; his
handshake will be light and hasty.

An unsure as opposed to a definite 'no' has a
very different nonverbal pattern. The client
will keep looking at you as he states the
refusal, turned towards you, head on one side.
He wants to be convinced, so he wants to
keep contact, to see more of you and hear

more of what you have to say. It is worth while trying to convert this into a yes.

When you get that yes, look for just how definite it is. Do you still see signs of uncertainty? If so, check out what the client's reservations are. But if you see direct eye contact, an unambiguous nod of agreement, a smile of reassurance and a prolonged and definite final handshake, then celebrate. You have made the sale.

## What Are People's Hidden Agendas at Meetings?

Everyone has her (or his) own aims and goals in a meeting – and most people mix and match. If someone has a particular agenda, you may find that her nonverbal behaviour follows a particular pattern.

Who arrives on time, eager to start, willing to chat but only to the people who might be useful to her during the meeting? She is the one who will be most keen to get things done, least likely to get distracted. Who arrives slightly early, in company with others that she has already met before the discussion starts?

She is likely to consider people important and be wary of any decisions that alienate staff. What about the latecomer? If she is calm and unhurried as she arrives, then the meeting may not be all that important to her. But if she makes an entrance and demands attention as she comes in, then her lateness may be a powerplay; watch out for her attempts to gain control during the meeting.

Where do people naturally sit? If placings are not predetermined, then the person who gravitates to the central point of a long side of a meeting table will be most likely to take everyone into account – though she may also have the most control simply by being best able to see what is happening. 'End sitters' like to get things done, often by directing or sometimes by bullying the team; their second-in-commands often sit just 'round the corner' from them. Opponents often make sure they sit opposite each other, while those who work together are often, quite literally, 'on the same side'.

What do people concentrate on during the meeting? A 'people person' will keep looking and listening at other delegates; you may actually see her head turning, as if during a tennis match, to get as much input from other participants as possible. Someone who utilizes objects as 'props' – opening a folder, waving a piece of paper, slamming down a glass – may well be interested in control; she will focus on objects because things are more manageable than people are. And the delegate who focuses on the agenda and the clock at the expense of everything else will be someone who wants to get things done.

When it comes to leaving the meeting, each delegate will have her or his own style. The 'getting things done' delegate checks in briefly with the people she needs to do business with, waves a general goodbye to others, and leaves quickly to be on time for her next meeting. Someone who wants to be in control of the situation will say goodbye only to the higher-status people, with a light touch or handshake; research suggests that touching people in a power situation makes them more manageable. The 'people person' too will touch, but in a sociable way – an arm touch, a friendly hug or (for women) a kiss on the cheek. This delegate will make sure to say goodbye to everyone in the room and will exit with a friendly smile.

## How Can I Use Body Language to Help Meetings Go Well?

What is said at meetings is only the tip of the iceberg. Underneath lies a whole layer of body language signals that can alert you to delegates' thoughts and feelings. If you are leading a meeting – or are in a position to influence it – then you can act as soon as you read these signals.

Who is really involved, and who is just marking time? A delegate who leans forward with his legs drawn back under him, whose head is alertly tilted and whose eyes open slightly wider in response to a key point is genuinely interested – while one who leans back with his legs stretched out, his head turned away or demonstrating a total lack of eye movement is not really feeling involved or absorbed. You might want to draw that delegate into the discussion by inviting him to speak, and then rewarding his contribution with the natural human 'acknowledgement' signals of a slight smile and the occasional slow nod.

At the other end of the scale, what about someone who wants to contribute? You may notice such signals as direct and fixed eye contact with the chairperson to try and make contact; an irritated expression with lowered brows; a sharp intake of breath as if preparing to speak; or a raised finger or pen – a gesture that survives from having to raise a hand to speak in school! If you do spot these signs,

look fixedly at the delegate who is giving them
– that will focus other people's attention, and
will ensure that the delegate is heard.

Who agrees with whom? Body language often
reflects mental approach, and you can often
tell which people are on the same side because
they may be sitting in the same sort of posture
and using the same kind of gestures. If one
person moves and another shifts position
directly afterwards, then you can be pretty
certain that they are broadly in sympathy. If
one of them then changes to copy a member
of the opposing 'team', then you need to be
prepared for a transfer of loyalty!

Outright disagreement is easily spotted:
people frown, shake their heads and shout!
But watch too for early signs of rising
irritation. Glancing away can reveal

impatience – literally an unwillingness to see the other person and his point of view. Lowered eyebrows and pursed lips reflect ape 'anger' signs, and can spell trouble. Crossed arms can mean a defensive attitude (though they can also mean a cold room!). In all these cases you may well want to use a calm tone of voice and soothing gestures to compose the meeting – or a sharp firm tone and decisive gestures to bring the delegates to order.

Lastly, as the meeting nears its end, it is worth checking that decisions have really been agreed by everyone in the room. If when you review proposed action people look away or shift in their seats, this shows they are unsure or will not in practice back your plan. Keep the discussion going until, when you summarize the agreements, you see delegates

looking at you steadily and giving a slight nod
– this means you have their agreement, and
their co-operation.

# How Can I Recognize
# a Liar in Business?

Recognizing when business contacts are aware of something 'wrong' in what they are saying is fairly easy; there are clear signals that reveal this. The problem is that in business people can give out such signals for reasons other than that they are lying. They may be telling the truth, but know that what they are saying will be unwelcome. They may be telling the truth, but not really want to be telling it. So read the nonverbal cues you see within the context of the situation you are in. That said, when someone says something that she knows to be 'wrong', a number of things are obvious. First,

her body finds it difficult to allow her to
speak. She may put her fingers slightly across
her mouth, as if to stifle the words. She may
use the 'choker' gesture in which the hand
goes to the throat, as if to stop herself
speaking. Even if she does not do this, her
throat muscles may close so that you may hear
a slight rise in pitch or vocal tremor. If the
words do come out, they may do so in a
confused way: the person may stutter,
hesitate, mumble, switch words or sentences
around, or get halfway through one phrase
and then switch to another.

Also, a liar's body, aware of all these give-
away signals, may try to mask them. So a
person may deliberately 'blank out' her body
language: she will turn away slightly, or turn
her head to one side; she will stand unusually
still; she will use fewer gestures than usual; she

will keep his expression fixed. Particularly, she may keep her hands still, and turned inwards – studies suggest that it is easier for people to fib if the palms of their hands are held downwards and out of view. She may try to show that she is unconcerned by direct eye contact and a bright smile, but end up using the 'false smile' which reaches the lips but does not engage the muscles round the eyes.

Underneath all this masking, a liar is nevertheless sending out all kinds of nervous signals because she is afraid of getting spotted. These signs will not easily be seen, and will not appear at all in those parts of the body that are most on show, such as the face. But far away from that 'centre stage', at the periphery of the body, a liar's fingers may be fidgeting, toes twitching, feet tapping as if trying to escape. And the unconscious, uncontrollable signals of stress, from the nervous system, will come to the surface regardless; so a liar may have uneven breathing, a tendency to clear her throat, a sudden change in skin colour, or a dry mouth that causes her to lick her lips more often.

If you do suspect that a colleague is not telling the truth, then often there is simply nothing you can do about it. Sometimes, however, it may be possible to challenge her by using body language which makes it more difficult for her to lie. The more directly and closely a person is challenged by another, the more uncomfortable she will be if she is lying. So move close, face your colleague directly, get eye contact, and take on a serious, unapologetic expression. Then ask your question again. This time, you may hear the truth.

## How Can I Defend Myself Against Sexual Harassment?

**W**hether you are a woman or a man, sexual harassment can be a problem. How can you avoid it?

Your first line of defence could well be to make sure that your appearance simply cannot be misinterpreted. The hard fact is that, particularly in a work context, sexy dress can attract unwelcome attention – and this applies to both sexes. Of course it is beyond argument that whatever you wear and whatever your body language, you have an inalienable right not to be sexually intimidated. Even so, some people interpret certain signals incorrectly, and therefore it is sound practice to leave at home the icons of sexuality, such as black leather, red lipstick, flowing hair, tight trousers or an open shirt, in favour of the icons of professional inaccessibility, such as tailored suits and a neat appearance.

Your second line of defence is awareness. If you can spot sexual harassment the minute it begins, then you have a much better chance of stopping it. So unless you want a relationship with a colleague, be wary of any behaviour that even hints at attraction. Take care if someone watches you constantly, gives you the overlong eye contact typical of a lover, comes within your intimate distance of 45 cm (18 in), or 'accidentally' touches you and then strongly denies that anything happened.

It can be difficult to react disapprovingly because to do so is so socially untypical. You may think that you are imagining what is happening; but even if you are, it is fairer on all concerned to signal immediately that you feel uncomfortable. So indicate your unease at these things as early as possible. Show that you feel invaded; step back out of intimate distance, fold your arms across your body and turn away. Show your disapproval by frowning, and speaking in a clipped and frosty tone of voice. You can nip suggestive behaviour in the bud by revealing your disapproval clearly at the start.

What if the worst happens? Suggestions are made, an accidental touch lingers, a hand is placed where it should not be. This kind of harassment is not about sex but about power, so the most effective reaction is a direct and powerful challenge. Do not smile and use a soft voice to reprimand, because this will make you seem apologetic. Do not just pull away and go, or your harasser will simply try again. Instead, react immediately and angrily. Pull yourself up to your full height, pushing your harasser back, speaking loudly to draw attention to what is happening. Say 'No, don't!'; 'How dare you talk like that to me!', or even 'Does this hand belong to anyone?' If you can both embarrass your harasser and make other people a witness to the embarrassment, then you may not have to make a formal complaint. You will have shown that you are as powerful as your oppressor, and you may never be troubled again.

# How Can I Handle a Difficult Boss?

What do you do with a difficult boss, one who gets irritated, angry, nervous or irrational? The problem is that you cannot simply react towards him (or her) in the way you would towards a friend – shouting back at his irritation, calming his nerves with a hug or a drink. For, to some extent, even with the most democratic boss you do need to maintain some remnants of what you might call 'subordinate' body language – respectful and unchallenging. So what can you do?

An aggressive boss, one who responds to pressure by shouting, making hostile gestures or even throwing things, can be very disturbing. He may not actually be angry at you – but he is aiming the emotion in your direction. Faced with your boss' aggression, your body may well quite spontaneously, and understandably, react with panic or with equal anger. So see to your own physiological needs first, breathing deeply in order to lower your heart rate and pulse rate, perhaps even carrying out a quick relaxation drill by tensing your whole body deliberately and then consciously letting your muscles slacken.

Then try not to increase your boss' aggression by confrontational body language. Look down at the desk rather than directly staring into his eyes, turn away slightly rather than taking up an aggressive posture with shoulders squared.

As soon as you can, say quietly but firmly that you are going to find some papers. Do not even look at your boss – for a permission which he may refuse – but simply leave the room and wait a few minutes to allow things to cool down. Then return with a friendly expression, behaving as if nothing has happened.

A boss who gets nervous or even panicky under pressure needs slightly different handling. Here his random gestures, shaky or distracted voice, pacing round the room or nervous habits will tell you that something has happened to put him off balance. What he does not need is for you to get disturbed by this – because then he will have to handle your panic as well as his own. So once again make sure you are imperturbable, perhaps going through the relaxation drill mentioned above.

You do not need to leave the room in this situation; if you do, your boss may feel unsupported. Instead, let your unruffled posture show that you are calm, and simply keep watching as he paces about. Psychologists suggest that giving others your attention, even if no words are spoken, may well actually relax them physiologically, so be prepared to do this for several seconds or even a few minutes. You will be able to tell that your boss is feeling steadier when his movements slow and he looks at you as if seeing you rather than seeing through you. This is the point at which you can start to offer practical help.

## How Can I Tell Whether I Am Doing Well in Work or Not?

It can be very difficult to assess what people really think of your work. Sometimes they do not know, sometimes they will not say. Sometimes the only way is to read their nonverbal signals, which are a direct line to their real judgement whether they know it or not.

So what if a manager or colleague approves of what you have done? The obvious signs are an approving smile, a tone of voice that rises with enthusiasm, a brief celebratory touch on your shoulder or arm. But a boss who is not a 'people person' may not feel comfortable doing any of these things, so what should you look for? The most basic approval movement in most cultures of the Western world is a forward nod; however restrained someone is being she (or he) will find it difficult not to give a tiny nod like that when she sees something that feels good to her. Equally, if something is satisfactory many people add a slow outbreath to the nod – not a shudder of frustration but a barely noticeable contented sigh.

You need to be careful, however. All the approval signs mentioned above can be faked by someone who does not dare tell you her real thoughts about your work. Watch particularly for a false smile, which unlike a real one starts and fades just too slowly, tends to get stuck at its widest point and, because it

does not use the muscles around the eyes,
never seems to touch the person's whole face.

Clear disapproval is fairly easy to spot; you do
not need body language skills to know when
you are being shouted at! You will probably
be able to recognize even mild disapproval
– a puckering of the forehead, the lowered
eyebrows of irritation, a faster tone of voice,
a short sharp outbreath. All these signs reveal
irritation and frustration.

But what if someone is not sure what she feels,
or dare not be clear about negative feelings?
Watch for the most basic disapproval
movement in most Western cultures, the shake
of the head. It is said to have developed from
the movement all humans use as babies to
refuse food by turning away from it – and is
often accompanied by the closed mouth,

pursed lips or slightly protruding tongue that a baby uses when she does not want to be fed!

The most useful response, of course, is to ask your colleague to say more about her reservations. And the most useful accompanying body language is the slightly tilted head and questioning glance that lets you ask a person, in the most unthreatening way, to say more about what she feels. Reassured that you are not going to get angry in return, the hesitant critic may well be persuaded to say you how you could improve. You may well end up gaining more approval for being able to handle feedback than disapproval for your original error!

## Are There Nonverbal Tactics I Can Use to Get Ahead?

**I**t would be nice to think that sheer talent and expertise gets you promotion. But in fact most people who are promoted fulfil one other key requirement: they act in ways that fulfil their company's unspoken criteria.

So look carefully at all the elements of your body language. You may want to read the sections of this book on dress (*page 26*), workspace (*page 22*), use of time (*page 52*) and person-to-person style (*page 31*). Aim to meet your company's criteria in all these areas, taking your model from the best

practice of the level you are already on, but also looking at what happens in the level above you – what is known as 'aspirational' body language.

Are you, for example, still dressing as if you are a junior? Should you be wearing a more expensive suit or more subtle makeup? The higher up the company you go, the more likely it is that you will be expected to dress expensively and stylishly – employees have been kept at their current level for decades because they insisted on wearing nylon shirts!

Does your workspace still look as if you are on a level lower than your own? Is there no computer in sight in a company where the top people get the biggest screens – if so, start throwing temper tantrums until you get one too. On the other hand, if the bosses have clear desks and only the typists use word processors, then you might wonder about keeping your computer firmly switched off, or even putting it back in its box!

Are you still organizing your time as if you were a worker rather than a manager – with most of your day spent doing the job yourself, when the company now wants to see you scheduling meetings to guide and brief other people?

In particular, how are you acting towards those above you in the company? You should not be aping them by using exactly the same nonverbal signals as they do – for that will threaten the hierarchy and people will automatically block your progress. On the other hand, be wary of being too subservient in the hope that it will curry favour.

Overpleasant, placating smiles, a syrupy tone
of voice and submissive body language may
make your boss feel superior to you, but it
will also make him see you as someone who is
naturally subservient. He will not be able to
imagine you being self-directed, taking
responsibility, or managing staff. As a result
he may find it impossible to conceive of you
ever moving up in the firm.

## How Might My Body Language Alter When I Get Promotion?

You have been appointed team leader or made manager. Of course this will cause changes in your job. And one of the things that you may notice changing is your body language. If you succeed as a leader, then quite spontaneously you will start putting out different nonverbal signs – the more authoritative signals of 'leadership'.

You may, for example, notice that you are more 'formal' with subordinates – even with people who used to be good friends. In order to manage them, you have to keep your distance somehow, showing colleagues less of what you are really thinking and feeling. So you may tend to control your posture, use more directive gestures, keep a more fixed expression, speak more deliberately and less emotionally.

You will also begin to use body language that shows that you have privileges. In a meeting you will sit more centrally. You will expect to talk first, talk longest, to interrupt subordinates and not to be interrupted by them. If you make a suggestion, you will expect it to be acted on. You will feel better able to move into a subordinate's space, enter without knocking, approach her (or his) desk more closely.

Interestingly, when dealing with superiors your body language may actually become more informal after your promotion, because you are now more their equal. Rather than being nonverbally 'on the alert' as if to do their bidding, you will find yourself sitting in a more relaxed way, smiling and laughing with them more, even touching them to make contact or offer support. They in return will be more relaxed with you, perhaps calling you by your first name, inviting you to the pub or to their house.

Is it possible to become a better manager by deliberately taking on 'leadership' body language? The answer is a definite maybe. If you do, then perhaps you will immediately feel more confident and begin to act that way naturally; confidence underpins all successful leadership body language. This may well work, particularly in a situation where you are managing people who do not already know you. Simply by adopting more formal and more 'privileged' body language you will start acting like a leader, you will encourage them to think of you as a leader, and they will.

But using the body language of a leader may backfire on you. You may find it difficult to maintain, and other people may find it difficult to accept – particularly if they used to be your friends or colleagues. They will react resentfully or mockingly, and you will struggle to keep control. So if you have been promoted to a new position within an old situation, you may have to allow your new, more authoritative body language to grow with the job.

Whichever route you take, if you are successful in your new role then a few months or years down the road you will almost certainly notice a shift in your body language. You will be acting like a boss – and other people will be treating you like one.

## How Can I Best Motivate My Staff?

Challenging jobs, increased pay packages, better working conditions – all of these are vital to job motivation. But studies have shown that the way you encourage or reprimand staff is just as big an incentive.

When rewarding staff, whether informally by a quick 'Well done' or formally with a certificate or medal, you will make them feel even better by using positive body language. Go right up to them, smile approvingly, give them just a few moments' complete attention to show that their contribution is important.

If appropriate – and only if appropriate
– mark your feelings by actual contact
– research done with sports teams reveals that
competitors, for example, felt even better if
congratulations were accompanied by a
shoulder slap or light touch.

Telling staff to do something differently
– or again – also needs appropriate body
language. All too often, because you feel so
frustrated, you can fail to re-instruct clearly,
or fail to check that the employee has
understood the re-instruction. So begin by
reducing your feelings of frustration or
irritation by consciously relaxing. Then, face
the employee directly so that you can see
each other clearly, but at a slight angle so
that he (or she) does not feel confronted.
Explain the problem.

Then, check from the other person's body language that he has grasped what you are saying. Are you receiving the clear nod of the head and eye contact that display understanding and agreement? Or are you getting the slight turn, glance away and dismissive gesture that signal that the employee resents what you are saying, or simply does not know what you are talking about? If the latter, you need to take action or explain your point more clearly.

What if staff need to be told clearly that they have done something wrong? It may be tempting to soften a disciplinary blow with gentle body language, but research has shown that a criticism accompanied by an apologetic smile or timid tone of voice creates resentment – employees think you are 'two-faced'. Instead, without getting angry, use body language appropriate to the occasion. Do not smile, do frown, do allow your voice to be serious. Such obviously disapproving body language will eventually lose its effect if it is your only way of behaving to staff, but will create the effect you want if you are the sort of manager who is usually even tempered and supportive.

Remember, finally, that once the disciplinary issue is over, it is important to let negative body language disappear – particularly if the employee's performance genuinely does improve. It can be tempting to keep a frosty air towards a 'culprit' for months afterwards, just to remind him of what might happen if he re-offends. But often all this does is to convince the employee nonverbally that he will never be able to get ahead in this particular company. And if he believes that, he will lose his motivation along with his job satisfaction.

# How Can I Hire the Best Employee?

Many employers judge job applicants on their interview presentation. But there is a problem here: Interview performance has been shown to have a direct link with success only in those jobs that involve interview skills. In other words, if you choose a applicant because she (or he) is confident and extroverted, she will only do a good job for you if that job depends on her being confident and extroverted. If not then she may not be able to do the job at all!

One way round this which more and more companies are using is as follows. List the qualities you are looking for – practical, mental, emotional. Then, rather than asking an interviewee whether she has these qualities (to which question she will, of course, say yes), give her a series of practical tasks. As she performs each task, check her skill by observing her nonverbal approach; this will give you accurate information about how she would actually perform in practice.

Say that job success depends on an employee's being methodical and organized. At the interview, present her with a box of mixed stationery and ask her to reorganize it – then observe closely. Does she recognize which objects should be grouped together; does she use paper clips and folders to gather objects; does she pile things neatly and straighten corners; does she leave anything in the box and forget about it?

What if a job depends on an employee's working to a tight deadline or under stress? Set a straightforward practical task, such as filing, and add a deadline that puts the applicant under time-pressure so that she probably will not finish however fast she works. What you watch for is not whether she completes the task – though you do not tell the applicant this. Instead, notice whether she becomes less or more effective as the minutes tick away; whether she starts to drop things and apologize; whether she simply slows down until there is no chance of finishing; whether she rushes through inaccurately in order to get the job done.

Do you want an employee to be co-operative in her approach to work? In that case, get her doing a task in tandem with someone else, explaining clearly that it is working together that is the key skill you are looking for. It is amazing how, even given that instruction, different applicants will react in different ways. Does the candidate cut the other person out with hostile gestures and sharp tones in order to complete the job herself? Does she urge the other person on with an encouraging expression on her face and tone of voice? Does she smile and chat in a friendly fashion – but at the expense of the task in hand?

Using body language as your crucial test is an accurate and effective way of finding out who can do a job – and who only says she can!

## How Can My Body Language Help Me Get the Job I Want?

So you are applying for a new post that will give you more of what you want – be it job satisfaction or hard cash! The first way body language can help is by showing you whether you really do want the job.

Nonverbal signals can give you high-quality information about your potential employer. As you take that pre-interview guided tour, look around at the architecture, the environment, the overall nonverbal style of the company (*see pages 18 and 22.*) Do the chipboard desks indicate a low-status

company – if so, how do you feel about that?
Do the partitioned workspaces hint that you
need to work largely on your own to survive
here – if so, will you fit in? Does the pace of
people moving along corridors suggest that
they are on tight deadlines – if so, are you
happy working under pressure? If what you
see puts you off, then in the long term you
may not be happy with the job. If what you
see excites you, then go for it.

As you move into the interview part of the
selection procedure, use body language again
to boost your self-presentation. For example,
it is obviously a good thing to be confident
during an interview; a steady approach makes
you better able to demonstrate your real
worth. So spend a moment calming yourself
by taking a deep breath and letting it out, by
tensing your muscles and then letting them

'flop'. Take up a confident position, sitting squarely on your chair rather than slumped to the back (which will make you look uninterested), perched on the front (which will make you look anxious), or angled unsymmetrically (which will make you look uncertain). Place your hands in your lap so that you will not be tempted to fidget nervously – though do not be afraid to make gestures to emphasize what you are saying.

As well as displaying confidence, also use the body language of approval. For research has shown that the body language patterns most likely to make interviewers feel positive about you are the ones that indicate you approve of them! So as they speak, acknowledge what they are telling or asking you: keep good eye contact, smile, nod when they say something you agree with.

Allow your body language – and your words
– to reflect what you have seen in the
company during your pre-interview tour. Of
course there is no point in lying, verbally or
nonverbally – in the end you either are or are
not the right person for the job. But if you
have spotted from existing employees' body
language that being a people person is what is
needed, mention your ability to get on with
others and work as part of a team. Then let
your body language demonstrate your
extroversion as you interact with those you
meet – interviewers and other staff alike.
Show them, as well as tell them, that you are
the right person for the job and that you
deserve to go far!

As you reach the end of your interview,
remember that recent research has shown that
the last impression you make is the one that

will stick most in interviewers' minds. So gather your belongings together efficiently, shake hands firmly, smile and make an unhurried exit.

Then wait for your letter of appointment ...